RAMPANT RUGBY LEAGUE

a guide to the greatest game

By David Walker

*Illustrated by Peter Hewlett
and David Walker*

LEAGUE PUBLICATIONS LTD

League Publications Ltd
Wellington House
Briggate
Brighouse HD6 1DN
England

First published in Great Britain in 2013
by League Publications Ltd

www.totalrl.com

© David Walker

A CIP catalogue record for this book is available
from the British Library

ISBN: 978-1-901347-29-6

Designed and Typeset by League Publications Limited;
Cover illustration by Honor James
Printed by Charlesworth Press, Wakefield

Thank you to my wife Suzanne and children Helena and Marcus for their help and support in the writing of this book. Special thanks also to Peter Hewlett for his support over the years and help with the illustrations.

INTRODUCTION

So what's it all about then?

There is this game called 'rugby', which is fair enough, but it is sometimes called 'rugby football'.

Are you like me and completely confused? If football is about kicking a round bag of wind in to a net and rugby is chucking a funny shaped ball about how can they both be called 'football'?

Not only that, there are two types of rugby football - rugby union and rugby league! So, if you have ever wondered why there are two types of rugby and especially what rugby league is all about, then this is the book for you.

With the help of a little bit of history, a little bit of geography and maybe even some maths we will find out about this sport called rugby league – is it rugby, is it football and, well, why are there two types of rugby?

Do not worry, the history or geography is not going to be too much like the stuff you do at school but it does involve some strange characters and some funny, true stories and you will find that some things you learn in this book will be useful at school one day. As for maths that will not be too difficult, it will only be things like why are there thirteen players in a rugby league team and fifteen in a rugby union team or what were over 102,000 people doing in

Bradford one May evening in 1954? They were not playing a giant game of tiddly winks, that's a fact!

Read on, because the story of how the different types of football, and rugby league football in particular, developed is a fascinating one and will explain many of the differences between the types of football we all know today. Some people know rugby players as 'egg chasers' but after you have read this book you will know there is much more to the game of rugby league than chasing an odd shaped ball.

HISTORY OF FOOTBALL

Why are there so many types of football?

So yes, it is a fact there are two types of rugby. That is not the end of the story, it would be a very short book if it were, in fact it is a bit more complicated than that. The two 'codes' of rugby are just two of the many types of football that have grown throughout the world and have become popular, not just with the people who play them, but with the hundreds of thousands who watch football in its various forms every week. But how did the different types of football begin in Britain?

We all know about football, eleven a-side with the aim to score a goal between the other team's goal posts. Top teams like Manchester United and Chelsea play this most popular form of football, or association football to give its proper name or 'soccer', a slang name for the same sport.

There is also American Football, Australian Rules Football, Gaelic Football, Canadian Football, Rugby Union Football, Rugby League Football and Bolivian square ball football (okay, the last one was made up). Although these games have some similarities they are all different, but they do have one thing in common, they all share the same roots.

WHEN PLAYING BOLIVIAN SQUARE BALL FOOTBALL, DON'T HEAD THE BALL.... THE CORNERS ARE REALLY HARD

13

All the following are clubs from one of the different types of football mentioned before, can you match up the club on the left with the type of football on the right?

1 Wolverhampton Wanderers   a. Rugby Union Football
2 Kilcock GAA   b. Australian Rules Football
3 Chicago Bears   c. Soccer
4 Sale Sharks   d. Rugby League Football
5 St Kilda Football Club   e. American Football
6 Sydney Roosters   f. Canadian Football
7 Edmonton Eskimos   g. Gaelic Football

How did you do?

1. Wolverhampton Wanderers — c. Soccer
2. Kilcock GAA — g. Gaelic Football
3. Chicago Bears — e. American Football
4. Sale Sharks — a. Rugby Union Football
5. St Kilda Football Club — b. Australian Rules Football
6. Sydney Roosters — d. Rugby League Football
7. Edmonton Eskimos — f. Canadian Football

The roots of football go back to the days when it was common on special days of the year, like Christmas Day or Shrove Tuesday for two neighbouring villages to play a game of 'football' against each other. However, this game wouldn't take place on the local park pitch; it is more likely there would be a 'goal' in each village, possibly several miles apart, and the aim would be to get an object, not dissimilar to a ball, into the opposing village's goal. Simple.

It was simple because there tended to be very few rules. Usually the 'ball' could be kicked, punched or carried; there was no restriction on the number of players and few rules on how to stop the goals being scored. Serious injuries were not uncommon and winning the game was very much a source of local pride. The games were played between those from the working classes, farm workers for example; it was not a game that gentlemen would play.

These games have been traced back as early as the sixteenth century and, in some cases even back to when the Romans were in Britain, that is nearly two thousand years ago. Therefore football of some form has been played in Britain for at least five hundred years and in some places, the tradition continues.

In Haxey in Lincolnshire, the 'Haxey Hood' is the 'ball' in a game played on the twelfth day after Christmas. Here a scrum of people push until the hood reaches one of four pubs in the village, where it stays until the next year. In St Colomb Major in Cornwall a silver ball is hurled around in a town versus country game every Shrove Tuesday, whilst in Workington, Cumbria over Easter several games are played with the goals at the town hall and harbour, about a mile apart.

Great, so there you have it. Football was born and that is why there are so many different types of football today.

Well, not quite. The problem was that if the rules for each game were different in different places how could teams play each other?

Then something really big happened that would have an impact on everyone and even these games of football - the Industrial Revolution.

You need to remember the Industrial Revolution, it will come in handy in history lessons in the future, when you can impress your teacher. Put basically, from the late 1700s there was more and more demand for all sorts of things like metals and coal which in turn were used to build things like trains and weapons and make textiles. Over this period a huge amount of inventions, often based on steam power, increased these requirements even further.

Some important inventions during the 1700s: -

1714 – Thomas Newcomen invented the first steam engine – used at first to pump water.

1740 – Benjamin Hunstman was first able to produce high quality cast steel.

1763 onwards – James Watt invented an improved steam engine good enough to power machinery in factories.

1764 – James Hargreaves invented the 'Spinning Jenny'. This allowed many spools of yarn (the thread to make textiles with), to be made at the same time. Before the Spinning Jenny this had to be done by hand and took a long time.

1774 – Claude De Jouffroy launched the first steam powered boat.

1784 - Andrew Meikle invented the threshing machine, which meant many fewer people were needed on farms to separate the grain from the stalks of wheat and barley. The grain was then used to produce flour.

Although many of the machines were built to make things easier, as demand grew, more and more people were required to work in the factories. At the same time 'common land' where people normally farmed was being 'enclosed' which meant these people were forced off the land and had to move to find work. They no longer had the land to keep their own animals or grow their own crops to eat. This meant small towns grew into huge cities as the people needed in these industries moved from the country to find work so they could earn money to feed their families. The power for these factories came mainly from steam and the steam was produced by burning coal. The large industrial areas began to grow where there was coal in the ground, places like Yorkshire, Lancashire and south Wales.

It was quite a revolution. Can you imagine? In the space of just a few years there were now hundreds of steam driven factories in the big cities all belching out choking smoke and soot. The people who worked in the factories ended up living in very poor housing, often in cramped conditions, a whole family in one room was not unusual with no toilets, no running water and no privacy, can you imagine what that would be like?

As the villages either disappeared under the expanding cities, or lost their young men to the cities moving to find work, the traditional football matches began to disappear as well.

THAT'S AWESOME!

Some of the biggest cities in Britain grew in population rapidly during the 1800s. For example in 1801, 94,421 people lived in Leeds, just forty years later this number was 250,000. It had grown in size by one and a half times in just forty years. This was repeated all over the country, other towns in Yorkshire that grew rapidly included Sheffield, which in 60 years increased in population from 60,000 to 220,000 - almost by four times. In seventy years the number of people living in Hull increased from 21,000 to 200,000 - increasing ten times.

Imagine if the number of people in your house increased ten times - it would be a bit of a squeeze.

So why was this not the end of football?

As industry grew, so did the wealth of the people who owned the factories and mines and the need for education grew in these 'middle classes'. The number of schools increased to educate the children of the businessmen, but it must be remembered at this time school had to be paid for and no one was forced by law to go to school. Children in the working classes were expected to work, they certainly could not afford to go to school. Whilst that might sound good now, the children had to work in dirty and dangerous places. They probably would have preferred to be in a classroom learning to read and write.

The middle class children whose parents could afford to send them to school had the time for physical exercise and this is where football comes back in to the story again. 'At last' I hear you say, all that talk of school was getting boring!

Many of the top schools had their own version of football by the 1820s and 1830s, most were 'handling' games, but involved kicking and some dribbling as well. However, this resulted in the same problem as the village football we talked about earlier – schools could not play each other because they each had their own rules which could be very different. So, for example, Eton School football had different rules to Rugby School football.

Hold on a second! Rugby School football, drop the school bit and you have rugby football – things are starting to fit together!

Slowly, but surely, during the 1800s, rules for football came closer together but as is often the case in these situations some people preferred one set of rules whilst others preferred another. Hence the people who used to go to certain schools wanted to continue playing soccer, so formed the Football Association or the FA in 1863, whilst the Rugby Football Union (RFU) was formed in 1871.

Even then the rules of both codes had more similarities than they do today – the original FA rules for example allowed the catching of the ball by anyone. Imagine if you could do that today –

> *"Manchester United attack up the left wing with Giggs, he reaches the goal line, surely he should cross to Rooney, he does......... and Rooney catches the ball before drop kicking it in to the back of the net, the goalie didn't stand a chance!"*

Some of the main differences between the two games that we know today were not so obvious then either, it was not until 1892 that the RFU stated that the rugby ball must be oval. In fact the codes were still very similar, so much so that some clubs that had been formed played both codes or swapped between the two.

Preston North End and Burnley, two famous soccer teams began playing rugby football before changing to soccer. Usually a newly formed club would choose to play the type of football that was most popular in the area. In Yorkshire the rugby code was very strong so most clubs in Yorkshire played rugby football.

A common story about the origins of rugby is that a boy at Rugby School, William Webb Ellis, picked up the ball and ran with it instead of kicking it during a game in the 1820s. As a result rugby football was born. However, the rules of football were such in those days that picking up the ball in any game of football would not be unusual. What would have been more unusual would have been if he had dribbled the ball down the field, done twenty five keepy uppies before performing an overhead cycle kick into the top right hand corner of the goal. It is a nice story though, but almost certainly made up.

THE BIG, BIG SPLIT

I'm not talking to you anymore; Why there are two types of rugby

As young men returned from their public schools and universities where they had enjoyed playing one of the two main types of football they began to form clubs in their home towns. Just take a look at the date that some of the top rugby and football clubs of today were founded or established and many of them will have a date in the second half of the nineteenth century. Arsenal's roots go back to 1886, Leicester Tigers were formed in 1880 and the club we now know as Wigan Warriors was formed in 1879.

'So that's the roots of football' I hear you say 'but why are there two types of rugby?'

Football was becoming more and more popular but at this time none of the players in either code were paid to play, they played for the enjoyment of the game and had jobs outside of the sport. They were amateur. No £50,000 per minute wages like soccer players seem to earn today!

However, in the summer of 1885, soccer (remember association football is its proper name) agreed to allow professionalism, in other words players were allowed to be paid to play. This came after pressure from many clubs, especially those in the northern areas of England, where they wanted to pay their players for playing the game. Many of the players worked in the factories and mines we mentioned earlier and could not afford to take time off work to play games. Most people worked long hours from Monday to Saturday and Sunday was for going to church. Yes, that's right people worked six days a week, not five days like today.

Up until this time most of the top clubs were made up of 'gentlemen' who could afford to play the game and had no need to be paid, however, professionalism had been creeping in to the game for some time. As a result 'Old Etonians' were the last amateur team to win the FA cup in 1882, beating the first northern club to reach the final, Blackburn Rovers.

In 1886 the Rugby Football Union, having seen the impact professionalism was having on its rival code, decided to protect itself. To their mind, soccer had let too many working class players into their game to the extent it was no longer a game played by gentlemen. They didn't want rugby football to go the same way and they were already starting to see a large amount of working class people in the rugby clubs of Yorkshire and Lancashire either playing or watching the game.

They introduced a new rule that said no player could be paid in 'cash or kind'. 'Kind' would be something that was not money but was worth something to the player such as food or clothing. If someone was found guilty of professionalism they could be suspended or even expelled from the game. The RFU had made things clear – no payment for playing rugby.

This upset the clubs in Yorkshire and Lancashire because the game was becoming very big in this area with large crowds paying to watch the top clubs. They were becoming businesses and to attract bigger crowds they wanted to win their games and have the best players. Many of the best players in the northern clubs were workers in factories, mills or mines. They had to take time off work to play and if they took time off work they did not get paid. So by playing rugby they were losing out on money to feed themselves and their families and to pay the rent for their homes. If you had to take time off work to play you would lose money - if you had rent to pay and had children to feed, what would you do?

The clubs in Yorkshire and Lancashire put forward a suggestion in1893 that instead of professionalism 'broken time' payments could be given to those players who had to take time off work to play. The vote at the annual general meeting of the RFU on whether to accept broken time payments turned down the idea. One of the main speakers against it, the Reverend Frank Marshall, even suggested those clubs who wanted to do this should break away from the RFU and form their own game. To some, Frank Marshall was the nasty man in this story, a snob who did not want common people playing the game of rugby football, to others he was the hero making sure that the game remained amateur and was kept away from the working classes.

THE REVEREND FRANK MARSHALL = SAINT OR SINNER?

AND WE DON'T MEAN DID HE SUPPORT ST HELENS OR SALFORD RED DEVILS

Just two years later on the 29th of August 1895, twenty two of the top clubs in Yorkshire and Lancashire had had enough of this situation. They met at the George Hotel in Huddersfield and voted to form the Northern Union (later to be called the Rugby Football League). By the 7th of September they had played their first round of matches.

Rugby football had split in two.

It was like you having an argument with your brother or sister about which channel to watch on television and as a result one of you going to another room in the house to watch a similar channel on a different TV......for the next one hundred years!

Each player in those first matches was paid six shillings (about 30p in today's money) but only if he could prove he was in employment and had lost a day's pay.

For the record those teams were: -

Batley, Bradford, Brighouse Rangers, Broughton Rangers, Halifax, Huddersfield, Hull, Hunslet, Leeds, Leigh, Liversedge, Manningham, Oldham, Rochdale Hornets, Runcorn, St. Helens, Stockport, Tyldesley, Wakefield Trinity, Warrington, Widnes and Wigan.

You may recognise some of the clubs as being rugby league clubs today whilst others disappeared a long time ago. The map below shows the location of all the founder members. The counties were very different from the counties you live in today, for example Lancashire is now split into different counties like Greater Manchester and Merseyside and Westmoreland does not exist anymore. As you can see the new northern union was concentrated in two main areas in the south of Lancashire and the west of Yorkshire, the only exception was Hull in the east of Yorkshire.

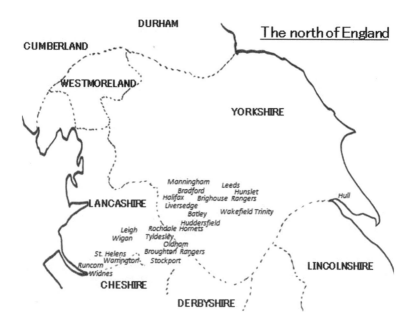

THAT'S AWESOME!

Probably the greatest example of the rise of working class men in rugby at this time was Dicky Lockwood. A labourer from West Yorkshire with limited education, he was a skilful three quarter who captained the England side in 1894 having made his international debut in 1887.

However, after a number of arguments with the Rugby Union authorities - including one occasion when he announced he could not afford to take time off work to play for England in Scotland - he switched to the new Northern Union game. Despite his try scoring feats for England – 5 in 14 matches, a record number of caps at the time – and his captaincy of England, he is rarely mentioned in official rugby union history.

Dicky Lockwood is a prime example of the prejudice that existed in rugby against the working classes at this time and shows why the split eventually happened. Unfortunately it all happened too late for Lockwood, he was declared bankrupt in 1897, in other words he had no money to feed or house himself.

Other than broken time payments made to players, northern union was very much the same game as rugby union at first.

However, the Northern Union realised that more paying supporters were needed at each game to pay the wage bill, so the game had to be more attractive to watch. Several rule changes were made quite quickly. In 1897, goals were reduced to be worth two points only and the line out was taken out of the game. By 1906 a tackled player would 'play the ball' rather than a ruck or maul being formed and the teams had been reduced to thirteen a-side from fifteen.

The players removed from the team were the wing forwards, also known as flankers. This position was seen as a 'spoiler' to open play; normally big but quite quick players they were the first men out of the scrum and could quickly stop the ball from moving across the field once it came out of the scrum. The game was suddenly faster and more spectacular to watch and was now similar to the game that is played today.

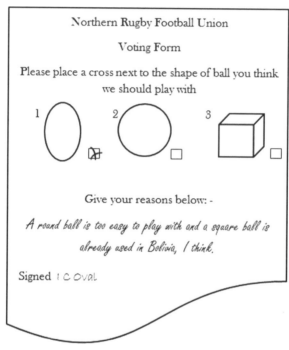

The Northern Union looked at other changes to rules as well, they even considered changing the shape of the ball.

THAT'S AWESOME!

The total wage bill in the first year of the Northern Union for St Helens was £106

The impact of the split on rugby union was huge at first. In August 1895 there were 416 adult rugby union clubs but by 1905 there were only

155, with just five in Yorkshire (there had been 147 in 1895). You don't have to be good at maths to know that was a big change, a lot players were now playing northern union instead of rugby union.

The England rugby union team was badly hit as well, in 1899 they were thrashed by 26 points to 3 by Wales, a defeat many blamed on the split as the northern teams provided a lot of the forwards for the international team. Eleven years earlier in 1888 the 21 man British squad selected to tour Australia and New Zealand contained fourteen players from clubs that would form the northern union.

The problem of professionalism did not go away for the RFU with the split, and during the next 100 years there were many stories and rumours of the amateur rules being broken. In fact one of the current top rugby union clubs, Leicester Tigers were nearly expelled from the RFU in the early 1900s after other clubs claimed they were paying their players.

There were often stories of players being banned from playing rugby union because they had played rugby league, however one of the more bizarre bans was a police team who played a charity rugby union game in 1896 on Huddersfield's Fartown ground. As they had played on a professional ground, the Rugby Football Union declared all the players were professionals and they were banned from playing rugby union ever again.

That seems a little unfair as they did not even play the new game of rugby. Any player who played northern union was banned from playing rugby union for life and this rule remained pretty much in place until 1995, often with amusing stories of players wanting to try the northern game playing in disguises or with false names – A.N. Other and John Smith were regular players in some rugby league games right up to 1995.

Ronnie Cowan played rugby league for Leeds in the 1960s but when he returned home to coach union club Selkirk, he was not allowed on the pitch as he was a professional. As a result he had to coach his team from behind a hedge!

THAT'S AWESOME!

Rugby league was born out of giving working class men the chance to play rugby; it has also given the chance for them to succeed in other ways as well. Cec Thompson is a fantastic example of how the game can help someone achieve great things.

Brought up in an orphanage, Cec had very little education and had little chance of getting anything more than very low paid work as a result. He left school at the age of fourteen barely able to read or write, he probably would not have been able to read this book. It was the 1930s and Cec was black in a time when black people were often abused in this country, just for the colour of their skin.

He then signed for Hunslet Rugby League Club and within three years he was an international for England. Whilst playing he also had a window cleaning round and he also decided to catch up on his education. He eventually obtained a university degree and became a teacher whilst he built up his window cleaning round in to a huge cleaning business employing 250 people. Cec believed none of this would have been possible without his rugby career that gave him the extra money, the friends and the self confidence to do these things. In addition to this he was one of the first black men to be a successful sportsman in the United Kingdom.

THE EVEN BIGGER SPLIT

That's it; I'm really not talking to you anymore, not for a hundred years!

By the early 1900s it was recognised that there was a need for international rugby league. Before the split of 1895 there had been regular international rugby matches, the first international rugby union game was between England and Scotland played in Edinburgh in 1871.

In 1907 something happened which would help maintain rugby league's presence for the future – a tour of Britain by a team representing New Zealand. The tour also included matches in Australia where it sowed the seeds for the game of rugby league in that country. Over one hundred years later, rugby league is as popular in some parts of Australia as soccer is in Britain.

THAT'S AWESOME!

The first international under rugby league rules was between Wales and the New Zealand 'All Golds' at Aberdare. Wales won 9-8 before a crowd of nearly 20,000.

Rugby union had been played in New Zealand for some time and the first tour by the New Zealand 'All Blacks' to Great Britain had been in 1905/06. Many of the players on this tour were persuaded by Albert Baskiville to join a tour to play the northern union teams in 1907. It was a big risk for those players taking part; they had to pay for their own clothing, hotel and travel expenses with a £1 per week allowance once they arrived in Britain. They had to pay for places to stay, food and transport for the whole team during the tour. If there was still money left over from the amount people paid to watch the matches they played in Britain, this amount would be split equally between the members of the tour. In other words if the tour was successful and lots of people came to see them play the players would make some money, if it was not a success they would lose money.

The prospect of the players being paid to play rugby did not go down well in New Zealand and the papers there nick-named them the 'All Golds' as they were seen to be professional rugby players and playing to be rewarded with 'gold'.

The tour was nothing like the short tours of today. There was no hopping on a jumbo jet and arriving twenty four hours later, the first flight in an aeroplane had happened only a few years earlier and it would be many years before a plane would be built that could fly around the world. The journey to Britain by sea took about a month with the team finally playing their first game in October 1907 against Bramley. This was the first of 35 matches on the tour with the final game against St Helens in February 1908.

THAT'S AWESOME!

The first tourists, the New Zealand 'All Golds' won nineteen of their thirty five tour games in Britain in 1907/8 and drew two of them.

On the way back to New Zealand the tourists stopped off in Australia, where the New South Wales Rugby League had been formed, and played several more matches, including three matches against Australia under northern union rules. International rugby league had been established in four countries – England, Wales, New Zealand and Australia – as a result of the All Golds tour. What's more, the tour had been a success off the field and each player received £300 as their split of the profits, a decent amount of money in those days.

However the game did not spread that rapidly after the All Golds tour. With a few teams already playing northern union rules in Wales by the time the All Golds toured, it was not until the 1930s that another international force became established – France.

French rugby union teams began to be formed in the 1880s and by 1923 there were almost 900 clubs, a huge proportion of them were in the south west of the country around Bordeaux and Perpignan. The game continues to be very popular in this area today. The RFU however, saw two problems with the game in France during the late 1920s and early 1930s. Some French clubs were paying their players and making little effort to hide this fact and there was a growing problem with violence both on and off the pitch. By 1931 things had got so bad that the English, Irish, Scottish and Welsh rugby union international sides decided they would not play France again until things got better. The Rugby Football League (RFL) saw this as a great opportunity to introduce their game to France and on New Year's Eve 1933 10,000 people in Paris saw the first rugby league match on French soil between England and Australia.

The first ever try scored in French rugby league was memorable for another reason. It was scored by Loys Van Lee for QEC (Paris Student Quarter Club) against Sport Olympique de Paris (SOP). As many players who tried their hand at rugby league risked being banned from other sports for being professional sportsmen Van Lee, a schoolboy athletics champion decided to disguise himself; with a beard and wig. A SOP player made an attempt to tackle Van Lee as he scored the try grabbing at his collar but instead he got hold of the bottom of his wig and pulled it off, the tackler fainted thinking he had pulled Van Lee's hair off!

The French quickly assembled a team of disgruntled rugby union players to tour England in 1934 playing northern union, or as it was now known, rugby league rules. Although the French won only one game on their six game tour the Ligue Francais de Rugby á Treize formed in the same year with ten clubs taking part in 1934/5. By 1939 there were more than 200 clubs in France.

THAT'S AWESOME!

The French national team won their first game of rugby league against Hull FC in a tour during 1934 by 26-23.

Then something rather large got in the way - the Second World War. War was declared on September 3rd 1939 and by June of 1940 the Germans had defeated the French and France was split into two zones by the Germans – the occupied zone (in the north) and the unoccupied zone (in the south). The French government moved from Paris to Vichy and effectively governed alongside the German occupiers. The Vichy government decided all sport in France should be amateur and promptly banned professional sport in general and especially rugby league. After the war rugby league re-established itself in France and was particularly strong in the 1950s, with two touring sides defeating the Australians in test series during that decade.

THAT'S AWESOME!

Jean Galia was the main person behind bringing rugby league to France and also played a major role in forming the Toulouse club, a town where he also had business interests. It is believed he, like many players at the time, was involved in the resistance during the Second World War. This was a secret organisation that fought against the German occupiers from within France. Galia ensured many people reached the safety of nearby Spain.

Being picked to represent England or Great Britain on a tour of Australia or New Zealand was seen as the greatest moment of a player's career and these tours became regular. However it meant the players had to spend a long time out of the country when selected for a tour in the first half of the 1900s. The journey had to be by sea as there were still no aeroplanes that could carry passengers all the way around the world. The 1928 tour left Tilbury docks near London on the 20th of April and did not arrive in Melbourne until the 28th of May. After that the players had to get down to the business of playing. In 1928 they played 28 games before returning home on the 28th of August. On the way home they stopped to play two games in Canada before finally arriving in Liverpool on September 28th – they had been away for five months.

As far as we know none of the players on the tour left their house saying they were popping out to play some rugby only to return five months later. One thing is for sure if they did it is certain that their dinner would be rather burned!

The players were paid whilst they were away, on the 1924 tour the players received the following:

£1 allowance per week whilst on the ship
£2 allowance per week when they arrived in Australia
£10 moving on to New Zealand
£2 per week to the player's wife
Just under 40p for each child the player had under the age of 14
Finally a third of the profits from the tour shared equally amongst all the players. Over 350,000 people saw the tour games in Australia so the tour made a profit.

Money was worth more in those days, so although these amounts sound a bit like your pocket money today it was a reasonable amount for the players in the 1920s.

On board the ship must have been a bit boring and difficult for the players to keep fit. A tourist in 1924, Harold Bowman, wrote that;

"It is becoming difficult to carry through with the rigours of training, owing to the hardness of the decks and the intensity of the heat. We now have sharp walks and play tennis which is very good training. We also have a bit of ball practise with a large rope ball weighing about three stone"

A French man, Paul Barriere, who was also involved with the resistance during the Second World War, came up with the idea of a rugby league world cup and the first tournament was staged in France in 1954, with Great Britain defeating the French in the final.

The world cup has been staged regularly since in varying formats, with the 2008 tournament staged in Australia to celebrate one hundred years of the game in that country. As the hosts had dominated international rugby league in the past three decades they were expected to win the ten team tournament with ease. After they beat Fiji in the semi final, Australia played New Zealand, who had defeated England in the other semi final. The crowd at the final in Brisbane did not expect to see the Kiwis record a convincing victory over Australia to win the world cup by 34 points to 20.

Rugby league's international development has stuttered along since the big breakthroughs in Australasia and France and for long periods the focus has been on club rugby, meaning international development has been left behind. However, there are domestic competitions and national sides for most of the Pacific Islands such as Tonga, Samoa, Fiji and the Cook Islands.

In addition there are similar set ups in countries where rugby union is also strong like South Africa and Italy and countries that have a large

Rugby League World Cup winners and runners up		
Year	Winners	Runners –up
1954	Great Britain	France
1957	Australia	Great Britain
1960	Great Britain	Australia
1968	Australia	France
1970	Australia	Great Britain
1972	Great Britain	Australia
1975	Australia	England
1977	Australia	Great Britain
1988	Australia	New Zealand
1992	Australia	Great Britain
1995	Australia	England
2000	Australia	New Zealand
2008	New Zealand	Australia

Australian or British connection like Malta, the Lebanon and Jamaica. The USA qualified for the 2013 world cup and they regularly play their near neighbours, Canada. There are also a number of nations in Eastern Europe playing rugby league such as Serbia, Latvia and Russia. Players in Super League play for several countries other than England, Scotland, Ireland and Wales. Jarrod Sammut, the Bradford Bulls scrum half, for example, plays international rugby league for Malta.

There is one country in the world where rugby league is the national sport; Papua New Guinea, a large island to 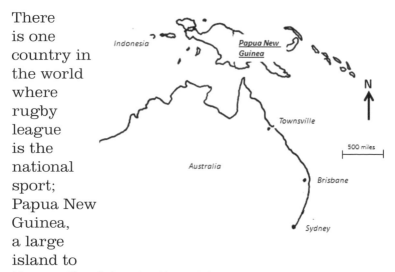 the north of Australia. This map shows where it is, close to Indonesia in the south Pacific.

Papuans are very passionate about their rugby league and have been known to walk for days to get to see the big matches in Port Moresby, the country's capital.

The game is taught in all schools and a huge proportion of the population are registered as players. Stanley Gene, Marcus Bai and Adrian Lam are three of the most famous Papuan players having made their names playing in Australia or England.

When Stanley Gene came to the UK to play for the first time he could speak very little English and the flat he lived in was very different from his house in Papua New Guinea. He said;
I can remember looking around and thinking I'd really made it. I had never had a cooker before, or a freezer, or even a power light...and we had a proper toilet that you could flush.

Can you imagine what it was like not to know the language and be at the other side of the world in a place very different to what you are used to? Not being able to understand the language did cause Stanley problems at first. Going fishing for the first time he took some advice from a friend;
'It's all in the cast. Throw it as far as you can.'

I followed his instructions....I wasn't sure what he meant by cast, but I threw it as far as I could. The whole rod.

As well as the world cup there are several other international tournaments, one of which is the Four Nations. This is played every year between England, New Zealand, Australia and either the European champions or the Pacific champions. In 2011 Wales joined the other three whilst in 2010 it was Papua New Guinea and the year before that France.

The 14th world cup was held in England and Wales in 2013 and the teams that competed were: - *Australia, Cook Islands, England, Fiji, France, Ireland, Italy, New Zealand, Papua New Guinea, Samoa, Scotland, Tonga, United States of America and Wales.*

THE NEXT ONE HUNDRED YEARS

It's a long time and some important things happened in rugby league

Rugby league became a popular sport and the gap between it and rugby union became too big for it ever to be merged back again. The argument with your brother or sister about which television channel to watch had now gone so far you are now in different houses, not just different rooms!

Rugby league did however have some very specific regional strength particularly Yorkshire, Lancashire and Cumbria in England and the south west of France. Many attempts were made to establish the sport in other places throughout the 1900s with teams in London being formed several times. In the 1930s there were two London teams and the Challenge Cup final was moved to Wembley in London at the end of the 1920s.

In 1980 another London club was established, this time playing at Craven Cottage. They were called Fulham and then went on to play at many different grounds around the capital and change their name several times – to London Crusaders, Harlequins RL and their current name London Broncos.

THAT'S AWESOME!

Jack Harrison is the only rugby league player to have been awarded the Victoria Cross, an award to recognise bravery in the armed forces. He still is the club record try-scorer for Hull FC in the 1913/14 season with 52 tries in one season, but he enlisted as an officer in the army when the First World War broke out in 1914. In 1917 second Lieutenant Jack Harrison of the 11th battalion East Yorkshire Regiment led his platoon against an enemy opposition. With just a pistol and hand granades he dodged gunfire to score a direct hit and silence a machine gun post. Unfortunately he was shot as he did this and killed. The winner of the rugby league competition between the Army, Navy and RAF is presented with the Jack Harrison trophy and there is also a memorial outside Hull's KC Stadium in memory of Jack.

Throughout the 1900s there was a steady drift of players from rugby union to rugby league tempted by payment to play a game similar to the one they played just for enjoyment. Many came from south Wales where the towns and industries were similar to those in Yorkshire and Lancashire. There were successes and failures, with some of the greatest rugby league players of all time originally being rugby union players. Two of the most recent successful 'converts' were Jonathan Davies who was a Welsh rugby union international before he signed for Widnes, and Martin Offiah who played union in London before also being signed by Widnes. It was a big decision to make because once a player had played a game of rugby league he was seen by the rugby union governing body as being professional and would be banned from rugby union for life.

Harold Edmondson was the youngest player to play first class rugby league when he made his debut for Bramley against Bradford Northern in 1919 at the age of 15 years and 81 days.

In the 1900s rugby league clubs in England played in various competitions but the two most important, as is the case now, were the Championship and the Challenge Cup. At different times clubs have dominated the game, with Hunslet winning all four trophies available to them in the 1907/08 season, probably being the first club to dominate the game.

THAT'S AWESOME!

The first Challenge Cup final to be played at Wembley was on the 4th of May 1929, when Wigan beat Dewsbury by 13 points to 2.

In 1941, during the second world war, Huddersfield beat Castleford in a cup match in very strange circumstances, what were they?
a) Castleford scored three tries and Huddersfield did not score any but won the game by getting more points from penalties.
b) The game ended 3 all after normal time and extra time had to be played, but the Castleford team were wanted back at the local army barracks for duty so Huddersfield had to play extra-time against nobody, kicking off, scoring a try to win the game.
c) Huddersfield won by a then world record of 100 points to nil.

ANSWER - b, it was in the middle of the Second World War and although many teams kept on playing a lot of players were in the army at near-by barracks. The war was more important than rugby so the Castleford players had to leave before extra-time could be played

After the Second World War, the game saw a boom in its popularity helped by increased national television coverage by the BBC. Crowds were huge, the championship finals (the 'grand final' as we call it now) and challenge cup finals were watched by crowds of more than 60 and 70 thousand and it was estimated that almost half a million people attended the games of the 1948 Australian tourists.

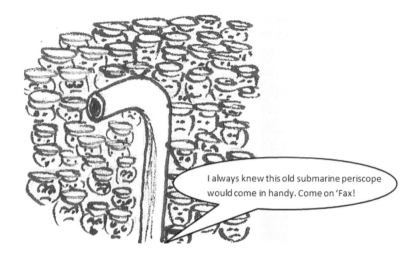

The biggest attendance in England at any type of football match outside of London was recorded in May 1954 when 102,569 watched the Challenge Cup final replay between Halifax and Warrington at Odsal stadium in Bradford. It is said the crowd was even bigger than that as many people got into the game without paying as the normal entry points were overwhelmed by the numbers of people. Warrington won 8-4.

During the 1950s and 1960s Wigan, St Helens, Leeds and Wakefield Trinity were the top clubs with all of them regularly appearing at Wembley during that period or winning the championship.

However, during the 1970s the game was beginning to decline in popularity and crowds were getting smaller. This was the decade when Widnes were called the 'cup kings' as they dominated the various competitions. The RFL took the bold decision in the 1970s to become the first sport to play on a Sunday afternoon and all the matches switched to kick off on that day of the week. Up until now Sundays had been days when nothing much happened – the shops did not open, there was no sport played and there was not a great deal on the television.

With both Hull FC and Hull KR starting to dominate the game in the late 1970s and the huge crowds that rivalry generated, the game began to gain in popularity again with regular sell outs for the cup final at Wembley, not least in 1980 when the two Hull teams met each other for the first time in a final.

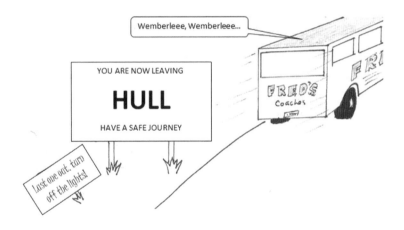

The team who have won the Challenge Cup the most times is Wigan. They have won the competition regularly throughout its history, but from 1988 to 1995 they never lost a cup game, winning the final eight years in succession. At the same time they won the championship seven years on the trot. During this period Wigan dominated the game more than any other club has ever done. If you were a Wigan fan this was a great period to support your team, however for fans of other teams it was a bit boring, it was like going in for school dinners every day and having the same food....for eight years!

THAT'S AWESOME!

Substitutes were only allowed from 1964 and only for injuries before half-time. From 1969 substitutes could be made for any reason and now the rules allow for up to ten 'interchanges' in a match, once a player has gone off the field he can go back on again unlike soccer or rugby union.

The Challenge Cup final has been a special day in the rugby league year since it moved there all those years ago. A day out in London at the fantastic stadium is great fun and 80,000 people do it every year. The final is now played at the new Wembley, but the finals from 2000 to 2006 were played elsewhere whilst the stadium was rebuilt. The winners and runners up (the beaten finalists) for the last twenty years are on the next page, is your club in the list?

Up until 1995 most rugby league players usually had another job; they were 'semi-professional'. There was not enough money to pay all the players a wage large enough so they did not need to do any other work. It is interesting that Wigan's dominance ended in 1995 as this was a really big year for rugby league, one of the most

Year	Winner	Runner Up
2013	Wigan Warriors	Hull FC
2012	Warrington Wolves	Leeds Rhinos
2011	Wigan Warriors	Leeds Rhinos
2010	Warrington Wolves	Leeds Rhinos
2009	Warrington Wolves	Huddersfield Giants
2008	St Helens	Hull FC
2007	St Helens	Catalans Dragons
2006	St Helens	Huddersfield Giants
2005	Hull FC	Leeds Rhinos
2004	St Helens	Wigan Warriors
2003	Bradford Bulls	Leeds Rhinos
2002	Wigan Warriors	St Helens
2001	St Helens	Bradford Bulls
2000	Bradford Bulls	Leeds Rhinos
1999	Leeds Rhinos	London Broncos
1998	Sheffield Eagles	Wigan Warriors
1997	St Helens	Bradford Bulls
1996	St Helens	Bradford Bulls
1995	Wigan Warriors	Leeds Rhinos
1994	Wigan Warriors	Leeds Rhinos

important in its development. One hundred years after it was formed and under increasing financial pressure the RFL took the decision, after making a deal with British Sky Broadcasting (Sky TV), to change the season in which the game is played from winter to summer. Super League was born as a result of this change with the top clubs making up this elite division.

At the same time the RFU finally decided to allow professionalism into rugby union. At last you have patched up your argument with your brother or sister and quite often watch the same television programmes in the same room!

The Super League was therefore formed and this allowed the clubs involved to share the millions of pounds on offer from Sky TV to make sure all their players could be full-time professionals. After one hundred years since rugby league was founded the players could just concentrate on playing rugby. At the same time, amateur rugby league clubs (clubs where people just play for fun and do not get paid) began springing up all over the country. Often based at rugby union clubs who saw that running a summer rugby league team brought people into their club in the otherwise quiet months of summer. It also gave the opportunity for rugby union players to play rugby league without the threat of them being banned from rugby union for life – remember, until 1995 this is what would have happened.

It also meant some rugby union players who had started playing rugby league before 1995 could go back to playing union, and a lot did. The tables were turned with some of the top rugby league players being tempted to play rugby union for higher wages than they got in rugby league. Two of the most famous and successful being Jason Robinson and Chris Ashton. As with the move from rugby union to rugby league in the past, there have been plenty of failures as well.

THAT'S AWESOME!

I'm sooooo bored. They said a rugby league scoreboard would have lots to do, I should have been a cricket scoreboard next door, they have lots to do, but then they have to work all day.

HEADINGLEY STADIUM

1986/87 CHALLENGE CUP SEMI FINAL

HULL FC	0
HALIFAX	0

TIME PLAYED – 79:57

Since Super League began in 1996, only one game has ended without a try being scored. This was a 5-2 win for Salford over Harlequins in 2007. In 1987 the Challenge Cup Semi-final between Halifax and Hull FC ended nil-nil, in the replay there was just one try, Halifax winning the game 4 points to 3 to reach the Wembley final.

There are fourteen clubs in the Super League, all of them are in England except Catalans Dragons, who are from the south west of France. At the end of the season the top eight teams 'play-off', meaning they play each other in a knock out tournament, with the last two teams playing in the grand final at Old Trafford, Manchester United's stadium. The winners of the Grand Final are the Super League champions.

The winners and the runners up of the Grand Final since 1997 have been, as follows, with Leeds Rhinos dominating in recent years: -

Year	Winner	Runner Up
2013	Wigan Warriors	Warrington Wolves
2012	Leeds Rhinos	Warrington Wolves
2011	Leeds Rhinos	St Helens
2010	Wigan Warriors	St Helens
2009	Leeds Rhinos	St Helens
2008	Leeds Rhinos	St Helens
2007	Leeds Rhinos	St Helens
2006	St Helens	Hull FC
2005	Bradford Bulls	Leeds Rhinos
2004	Leeds Rhinos	Bradford Bulls
2003	Bradford Bulls	Wigan Warriors
2002	St Helens	Bradford Bulls
2001	Bradford Bulls	Wigan Warriors
2000	St Helens	Wigan Warriors
1999	St Helens	Bradford Bulls
1998	Wigan Warriors	Leeds Rhinos

As well as being champions of Super League, the winners of the Grand Final also qualify to play in the World Club Challenge, playing against the winners of the NRL Grand Final in Australia. This has been a regular fixture since 2000 and the winners and runners up in this game since then are below, can you work out which ones are the Australian teams?

Year	Winner	Runner Up
2013	Melbourne Storm	Leeds Rhinos
2012	Leeds Rhinos	Manly-Warringah Sea Eagles
2011	St George Illawarra Dragons	Wigan Warriors
2010	Melbourne Storm	Leeds Rhinos
2009	Manly-Warringah Sea Eagles	Leeds Rhinos
2008	Leeds Rhinos	Melbourne Storm
2007	St Helens	Brisbane Broncos
2006	Bradford Bulls	Wests Tigers
2005	Leeds Rhinos	Canterbury Bulldogs
2004	Bradford Bulls	Penrith Panthers
2003	Sydney Roosters	St Helens
2002	Bradford Bulls	Newcastle Knights
2001	St Helens	Brisbane Broncos
2000	Melbourne Storm	St Helens

There are now rugby league clubs in every county of England, but as you will have seen, rugby league has always been about inclusion, everyone getting the chance to play the game, no matter what their background, colour or religion. This has been the case for many years, with the first black coach of a club (Roy Francis) and the first black captain of a British national team in any sport (Clive Sullivan) many years before other sports.

Rugby league thrives elsewhere; the student rugby league was formed in 1967 by Andrew Cudburtson, Jack Abernathy and Cec Thompson (remember him). There has been a varsity match between Oxford and Cambridge Universities since 1981 and the Premier Division is the top league in student rugby league – University of Gloucestershire All Golds have a team in the Premier South. Rugby league became a recognised sport in the armed forces (the Army, Royal Air Force and Royal Navy) in 1994 and teams compete in the Challenge Cup.

A governing body was first set up for women's rugby league in the mid nineteen eighties and there has been a women's rugby league world cup since 2000, New Zealand winning the first three before Australia won it in 2013. In 2004 wheelchair rugby league was developed in France.

People without a disability can compete in wheelchair rugby league and England won the first wheelchair rugby league world cup in 2008, but France are the current world champions, winning the trophy in 2013.

The game of rugby league has come a long way since 1895 but it has never been frightened to do something different or to change the way things are done. Starting with 'broken time' payments and reducing the number of players in a team, through to moving the cup final to Wembley, match days to a Sunday or even the whole season to summer.

Rugby League Timeline

William Webb Ellis supposedly ran with the ball in a game of football at rugby school	*1823*	
	1830	King George IV dies and William IV becomes king
	1837	Victoria becomes queen after the death of William IV
The Football Association (FA) formed	*1863*	
	1865	American Civil War ends
The Rugby Football Union (RFU) formed and the first international match between England and Scotland played	*1871*	

	1876	Telephone invented by Alexander Graham Bell
Association Football allows players to be paid	1885	
	1886	The first car is sold by Karl Benz
The northern union splits from the rugby union and rugby league is born	1895	
Batley win the first Challenge Cup	1897	
	1901	Queen Victoria dies and is replaced on the throne by Edward VII
Rugby league teams reduced to 13 a-side and the 'play the ball' introduced to replace the ruck.	1906	
First international game of rugby league between the All Golds and Wales	1908	
	1910	George V becomes king
	1914	The First World War breaks out and lasts until 1918
	1918	Women were allowed to vote in the UK for the first time
First Challenge Cup final played at Wembley	1928	First television sold

First game of rugby league played in France	*1933*	
	1936	George VI becomes king
	1939	World War Two begins and does not end until 1945
	1952	Queen Elizabeth II becomes queen, in the same year Edmund Hillary becomes the first man to climb Mount Everest, the world's tallest mountain.
Over 102,000 people watch the Challenge Cup final replay at Odsal and Great Britain win the first world cup	*1954*	
	1961	Russian Yuri Gagarin becomes the first man in space.
Substitutes first allowed in rugby league	*1964*	
	1969	Neil Armstrong becomes the first man to walk on the moon
Great Britain win the world cup – the last time they have won the trophy	*1972*	
	1979	Margaret Thatcher becomes the first female Prime Minister of Great Britain

Fulham RLFC are formed, the first professional rugby league team in London since the 1930s. They later change their name to London Broncos.	*1980*	
Wigan win the Challenge Cup and are not beaten again in the competition again until 1996	*1988*	
	1990	Apartheid (the segregation of people based on the colour of their skin) abolished in South Africa
Professional rugby league in the UK moves to a summer season and Super League is formed. Rugby union allows professionalism for the first time	*1995*	
	2001	'9/11' terrorist attacks on New York and Washington in the USA
St Helens beat Catalan Dragons in the first Challenge Cup final to be played at the rebuilt Wembley stadium.	*2007*	
New Zealand win the world cup, defeating holders Australia in the final in Australia.	*2008*	
The 14th world cup held in the UK.	*2013*	

In professional rugby league in the UK there are now thirty six clubs spread across the country. See if you can work out which club is closest to you.

The Professional Rugby League Teams of England and Wales

Gateshead Thunder

Workington Town
Whitehaven

Borrow Border Raiders

York City Knights

Bradford Bulls
Keighley Cougars
Rochdale Hornets
Salford City Reds
Swinton Lions

Leeds Rhinos
Hunslet Hawks

Hull FC
Hull KR

Doncaster

Sheffield Eagles

Batley Bulldogs
Dewsbury Rams

Widnes Vikings

North Wales Crusaders

South Wales Scorpions

Oxford RL

Hemel Stags

London Skolars

London Broncos

University of Gloucestershire All Gold's

①– Warrington Wolves

② St Helens

③– Leigh Centurions

④ Wigan Warriors

⑤– Halifax

⑥ Huddersfield Giants

⑦– Castleford Tigers

⑧ Featherstone Rovers

⑨– Wakefield Trinity Wildcats

⑩ Oldham

71

THE PLAYERS

Who plays where and what do they do on a rugby league pitch?

Rugby League is played in teams of thirteen with four interchange players. The interchange players can go back on to the field once they have come off but a team can only use ten interchanges in a match and can only have thirteen players on the field at any time.

There are a number of positions in a rugby league team and some have names that do not apply to what they do anymore – they have not changed even though the game has. Each position has a number although a lot of teams use a squad numbering system which means the number on their shirt does not always apply to their position. Which position do you think you are best suited to?

The Backs

The 'backs' are so called because they play at the back of the field behind the 'forwards'.

1.   **FULL-BACK.** One of the easiest positions to remember on a field, the full-back stays behind the rest of the team when they are defending as a last line of defence. They are often called on to do last ditch tackles after an opposing player has broken through the defence. They are responsible for ensuring the defence is in place because, like a goal-keeper in soccer, they can see everything going on in front of them. They often have to be brave when tackling and catching kicks.

The full-back also makes an extra man in the line of attack and is more and more the type of player who can create opportunities and kick well. A good example would be Sam Tomkins, the Wigan full-back who is seen as one of the most exciting players currently in the game.

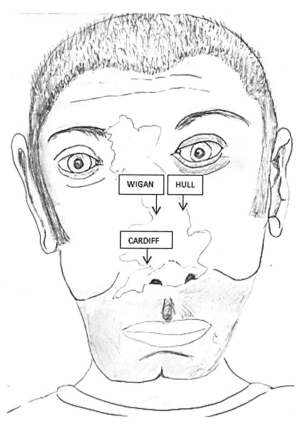

Shaun Briscoe, the former Widnes full back has broken his nose so many times it is now the exact shape of Great Britain. If you look carefully you can see the following places: - Wigan, his first club, Hull, where he played for both clubs and Cardiff where he would have won the Challenge Cup with his former club Hull FC had he not been rushed into hospital the day before the final with appendicitis.

2&5. WINGERS. These are the real speedsters in the team. There are two wingers in a team and they play on opposite sides of the pitch, they are also known as 'wing three-quarters' as they play three quarters of the way behind the forwards. Not only do wingers have to be quick, they also have to be able to tackle well and catch a ball in difficult situations. The opposition team will often kick to the corners to allow their wingers to catch the ball and score, so the wingers in defence have to be able to stop them from scoring by either catching the ball or tackling the player. The winger is also expected to do a lot of hard work 'bringing the ball up' where they catch a kick from the opposition team and then make as many metres up the field as they can before they are tackled. Tom Briscoe, the England winger, is one of the league's top scorers but he has saved many tries with his strong tackles as well.

Jamie Ainscough, a Wigan winger complained of an infection in his arm, an x-ray revealed a tooth embedded in it. The tooth belonged to Martin Gleeson, who had played against Ainscough for Warrington a month earlier.

Dear Martin,

Please find enclosed something that belongs to you. I have been keeping good care of it for you......

In my arm,

Love Jamie xxx

3&4.   CENTRES. Or 'centre three-quarters'.
centres are fast players as well and often score
a lot of tries, they have to be strong in defence
and form a good relationship with their wingers.
Often, it is a pass from the centre that allows
the winger time and space to score their tries.
Vincent Duport at Catalan Dragons scores lots of
tries for his club side from the centre position.

6.   STAND-OFF. One of two 'half-backs' in the
team, the stand-off or 'five eighth' is often called
a 'pivot' because a lot of the play revolves around
him. He is the link between the forwards and
the backs. Quick thinking and usually a good
kicker, the stand-off directs the team around
the pitch, deciding which way the ball should
go. Lee Briers at Warrington Wolves is one of
the best kickers in rugby league with kicks that
have got his club side or Wales out of difficult
situations and in to great attacking positions.

THAT'S AWESOME!

The highest number of points in a game was scored by Chris Thorman for York City
Knights in the third round of the Challenge Cup in 2011. Thorman kicked 20 goals
and scored four tries as his team completed a 132-nil victory over Northumbria
University. Thorman also holds the record for the fastest ever hat-trick of tries when
he played half back for Huddersfield Giants.

7.   SCRUM HALF. Another 'play maker' in the team the scrum-half is often quite small but fast over short distances. They usually are good handlers and passers of the ball as they often have the ball in their hands and decide where to pass it quickly. Danny Brough at Huddersfield is one of the smallest players in the Super League but is extremely strong for his size and very quick in tight situations.

Sean Long, the former St Helens scrum half, got a little bit excited after Saints scored a try in the last ten seconds of a Play-off game to beat Bradford Bulls;

In all the commotion, I pulled St Bernard's (the St Helen's mascot) big furry head off...I stuck the head on and ran across the pitch. I wanted to take the goal kick with the St Bernard's head on but the ref wouldn't let me.

Perhaps Sean had a great idea and all teams should wear their mascot's heads in matches.

The Forwards

The forwards tend not to be as fast as backs but they are usually bigger and stronger.

8&10.   PROP FORWARD. There are two prop forwards on the field at any one time but most teams tend to have two more as interchange players so they can give them a rest during a game. The props are the 'engine' of the team. They are used as a battering ram to take the ball up the field in the most direct route possible. That usually means running as fast as they can at the other team without holding back. However, when it comes to defence it is the props who have to do a lot of the hard work tackling the props on the opposition team. Eorl Crabtree at Huddersfield Giants is a typical, tough, no nonsense prop forward.

Take a very early bath Adrian

Adrian Morley, the new Salford prop, holds the unenviable record of the fastest sending off in an international match. He was sent off in the first test against Australia in 2003 when playing for Great Britain after just 12 seconds of the match, after a high tackle on Robbie Kearns.

9.   **HOOKER.** Traditionally the hooker was the player in the scrum who tried to hook the ball with his feet and win the ball for his team. Scrums in rugby league are very different now and the hooker no longer does this, in fact the hooker is now more like a half-back. He is usually the 'acting half-back' who picks up the ball after a play the ball – where a player plays the ball behind him with his foot after he is tackled. A hooker also tends to be quite small but fast and very strong. It tends to be the position on the field that does the most work, having to follow play to be at every play the ball but also to do a tremendous amount of tackling in the middle of the pitch as well. James Roby at St Helens is very fast from acting half-back and often catches the defending team out by running with the ball from acting half-back very quickly.

11&12. SECOND ROW FORWARD. Sometimes second row forwards do similar work to a prop and sometimes they take a wider position on the field to defend and attack in a position similar to a centre. They tend to be bigger than centres but still quite fast; it is not unusual for a second row to be able to play in the centres if required. Jon Wilkin of St Helens has scored many tries from at least forty metres showing how fast and strong he is.

13. **LOOSE FORWARD.** The last player to pack down in the scrum, the loose forward is often a play maker and a very good ball handler. They form a 'triangle' of playmakers with the scrum half and stand-off. In fact, the loose forward role can be very similar to that of the stand-off. Sean O'Loughlin, the England and Wigan loose forward, has played both positions during his career and is recognised as one of the world's top number thirteens. However, some teams might use a big player who normally plays prop forward at number 13. That way they have three 'battering rams' on the field at the same time – not much fun if you have to do the tackling against them.

Like any sport, it is not unusual for a son or brother of a professional player to also play the game at the top level.

Some of the best examples are the Tomkins brothers, Sam and Logan at Wigan (and their other brother Joel who used to play at Wigan) and the Burgess brothers. Luke, Sam and twins George and Tom Burgess are all professional players and their dad, Mark was also a professional. Jeff Grayshon did not retire from the professional game until he was 45 years old, by which time his son, Paul was also a professional at Featherstone Rovers.

Six weeks after James Leuluai scored two tries in the Challenge Cup final for Hull FC against Wigan, his son Thomas was born. Thomas Leuluai played for Wigan, whilst his cousin Kylie Leuluai plays for Leeds Rhinos, his uncle Phillip Leuluai used to play at Salford City Reds and his brother MacGraff plays for Widnes Vikings. Imagine if just two families combined to make one team.....

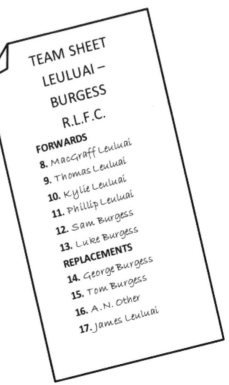

TEAM SHEET
LEULUAI –
BURGESS
R.L.F.C.

FORWARDS
8. MacGraff Leuluai
9. Thomas Leuluai
10. Kylie Leuluai
11. Phillip Leuluai
12. Sam Burgess
13. Luke Burgess
REPLACEMENTS
14. George Burgess
15. Tom Burgess
16. A.N. Other
17. James Leuluai

Finally, a game cannot go ahead without the officials, who have to make sure that both teams play to the rules of the game. The main official is the referee who makes all the key decisions on the pitch ranging from making sure teams are on-side, to awarding tries and in the case of extreme foul play, sending players off. In most matches he is supported by the Touch Judge, who can tell the referee if they see something he may have missed, in addition to their main tasks of judging where the ball goes out of play (in to touch) and whether a conversion has been scored. In some matches there is a Video Referee. When the main referee is not sure whether a try has been scored he can ask the video referee to take another look, using all the different camera angles available to him. When there is no video referee there is an In Goal Judge at either end of the pitch who helps the referee decide whether a try has been scored.

So what have we learned since 1895?

Rugby league has progressed a long way since the breakaway from rugby union in 1895 and even further since the days of villages playing football against each other across the open fields. It is now a fast, exciting sport to watch and play. Big occasions like the Challenge Cup final, Super League grand final and the World Cup final attract tens of thousands of spectators and millions of TV viewers. There is nothing more thrilling than seeing a player make a break into open space and the chase of the opposition players to try and pull him down before he scores. There is always a sense of anticipation as two of the biggest players on the field run towards each other, one of them trying to take the ball that bit further up the field, the other wanting to make sure he is stopped and goes no further.

We have seen that all forms of football developed from the same source and rugby league was no exception. For those involved in the game of rugby league there is always a sense of pride that it is a sport born out of wanting to give everyone the chance to play it, no matter what their background, and that it is one of the reasons why it is known as 'the greatest game'.

THE CLUBS

*Hundreds of facts
you might not
know about all the
professional rugby
league teams*

There are thirty six British clubs and one French club playing in the top three divisions in Britain – Super League, the Championship and Championship One. Now here's a quick guide to them, pay attention there is a test at the end!

BATLEY BULLDOGS

Year Formed	1880
Old nickname	Gallant Youths
Ground	Mount Pleasant
Biggest crowd	23,989 (v Leeds in 1925)
Champions	Once in 1923
Challenge Cup	Three times – 1897, 1898, 1901
Greatest moment	They were the first team to win the Challenge Cup.
Star man	Barry Eaton, who held the world record for kicking 38 consecutive goals in 2003, yes that's right in games between 29th of June and 24th August 2003 he did not miss any of his 38 kicks at goal.
Amazing Fact	Batley have played at the same stadium since they were formed – over 130 years.

BARROW RAIDERS

Year Formed	1875
Old nickname	Shipbuilders
Ground	Craven Park
Biggest crowd	21,651 (v Salford in 1938)
Champions	Never
Challenge Cup	Once – 1955
Greatest moment	Reached the Challenge Cup final three times between 1951 and 1957, winning it in 1955.
Star man	Willie Horne, who captained Great Britain to win the series against Australia in 1952, scored 113 tries and 739 goals for Barrow. There is a statue of him near the ground in Barrow.
Amazing Fact	Barrow were champions of their league (Lancashire senior division two) in the first year they played rugby league – 1897/8. .

BRADFORD BULLS

Year Formed	1964 – original club went out of business in 1963, originally formed 1907/08
Old nickname	Northern
Ground	Odsal Stadium
Biggest crowd	69,429 (v Huddersfield in 1953)
Champions	Six times – 1980, 1981, 1997, 2001, 2003, 2005
Challenge Cup	Five times – 1944, 1947, 1949, 2000, 2003
Greatest moment	Winning the World Club Challenge three times, the third time in 2006 beating Wests Tigers 30-10.
Star man	Trevor Foster, Great Britain and Wales international, he played 17 seasons for Bradford from 1938 and won every honour in the game. Even when he was 90 years old he continued to work at the club as official time keeper.
Amazing Fact	The Bradford club that was one of the founder members of the northern union, decided to switch codes in 1907, but to play soccer – they became Bradford Park Avenue and still exist in the lower leagues of soccer.

CASTLEFORD TIGERS

Year Formed	1926
Old nickname	The Glassblowers
Ground	The Jungle (Wheldon Road)
Biggest crowd	25,446 (v Hunslet in 1935)
Champions	Never
Challenge Cup	Four times – 1935, 1969, 1970, 1986
Greatest moment	Winning the Challenge Cup for the fourth time with a one point victory over Hull KR in 1986.
Star man	Malcolm Reilly, a loose forward who played for Castleford from the late 1960s to the mid 1980s. He was man of the match in the 1969 Challenge Cup final, and a member of the 1970 Great Britain team in that year's world cup. He played in Australia for Manly and was coach of Great Britain in the 1990s. He also coached Newcastle Knights in Australia.
Amazing Fact	In 2008 Castleford gave a trial to sprinter Dwain Chambers, he trained with them for a while and played in a trial game in a reserve team but decided the game was not for him.

CATALAN DRAGONS

Year Formed	2001
Old nickname	None
Ground	Stade Gilbert Brutus
Biggest crowd	18,150 (v Warrington at the Olympic stadium, Barcelona in 2009)
Champions	Champions of France, 2005
Challenge Cup	Runners up in 2007
Greatest moment	Playing in the first Challenge Cup Final against St Helens at the newly rebuilt Wembley.
Star man	Thomas Bosc, French international and former team captain, a half back who was also Catalans regular goal kicker making him the top points scorer at the club for several seasons.
Amazing Fact	The club were formed after a merger between two clubs based in Perpignan, St Esteve (formed 1965) and XIII Catalan (formed 1935) in 2001 and were originally called Union Treiziste Catalane or UTC for short.

DEWSBURY RAMS

Year Formed	1898
Old nickname	None
Ground	Crown Flatt
Biggest crowd	26,584 (v Halifax in 1920)
Champions	Once in 1973
Challenge Cup	Twice – 1911 and 1943
Greatest moment	Winning the championship against all the odds in 1973, winning the final after finishing eighth in the table.
Star man	Michael 'Stevo' Stephenson, now a presenter on Sky TV played for Dewsbury at hooker during their championship winning season on 1972/3. He was also a member of the 1972 world cup winning Great Britain side.
Amazing Fact	Eddie Waring, who went on to be a very famous BBC TV commentator, was the manager of the Dewsbury side during the Second World War. He cleverly put together a side using professional players from other teams who were serving in the army but based at a nearby camp (the rules at the time said a player could play for his nearest club whilst in the army). This ensured Dewsbury won the Challenge Cup in 1943.

DONCASTER

Year Formed	1951
Old nickname	The Dragons
Ground	Keepmoat Stadium
Biggest crowd	10,000 (v Bradford in 1952)
Champions	Never
Challenge Cup	Never
Greatest moment	Winning promotion to the top division of rugby league for just one season in 1994
Star man	Ellery Hanley, a former coach, but never played for Doncaster. He was one of the greatest players of the late twentieth century, playing for Bradford Northern and then Wigan when they dominated the game.
Amazing Fact	Doncaster regularly finished in the bottom three of the whole rugby league virtually every year from 1956 to 1985

FEATHERSTONE ROVERS

Year Formed	1921
Old nickname	The Colliers
Ground	Big Fellas Stadium (Post Office Road)
Biggest crowd	17,531 (v St Helens in 1951)
Champions	Once - 1977
Challenge Cup	Three times – 1967, 1973, 1983
Greatest moment	Winning the Challenge Cup for the third time in 1983 against hot favourites Hull by 14 points to 12.
Star man	Deryck Fox, one of a long line of scrum-halves to be produced by the club. He also represented Great Britain thirteen times whilst at the club in the 1980s. As with many players at the club he was finally tempted away to play at a bigger club, signing for Bradford Northern in 1992.
Amazing Fact	Despite the size of the town of Featherstone, it only has a population of 16,000, the club has had amazing success, winning all of the major competitions before Super League began and producing more than 30 international players. In 2010, 2011, 2012 and 2013 'Fev' finished top of the Championship, the division below Super League, making them one of the strongest clubs outside of the top division.

GATESHEAD THUNDER

Year Formed	1999
Old nickname	None
Ground	Gateshead International Stadium
Biggest crowd	6,631 (v Bradford Bulls in 1999)
Champions	Never
Challenge Cup	Never
Greatest moment	Winning the 2008 National League One, securing promotion to the Championship.
Star man	Ian Herron, Belfast born winger or full back, Herron kicked 105 goals in the 1999 season, a club record. He played for Ireland in the 2000 world cup.
Amazing Fact	Although only formed in 1999, this was not the first time rugby league was played in Gateshead. From the 1980s several senior and junior internationals were played at Gateshead as well as the Charity Shield, between the Champions and Challenge Cup winners.

UNIVERSITY of GLOUCESTERSHIRE ALL GOLDS

Year Formed	Late 1990s
Old nickname	None
Ground	Prince of Wales stadium, Cheltenham
Biggest crowd	553 (v Salford City Reds in 2013)
Champions	Never
Challenge Cup	Never
Greatest moment	Winning the British Universities Championship in February 2013, just before playing their first professional season.
Star man	Brad Hepi, coach of the All Golds, is a New Zealand born former professional player who has played for several clubs including Workington Town, Hull FC, Salford City Reds and Doncaster in the UK and Illawarra in Australia. His son, Tyla plays for the All Golds.
Amazing Fact	The All Golds play in Cheltenham which rightly claims to be the 'birthplace of international rugby league'. Do you remember Albert Baskiville and his touring 'All Golds'? They played against England in the third and deciding match of a three match series in Cheltenham in 1908 and won the match and therefore the series.

HALIFAX

Year Formed	1873
Old nickname	Blue Sox
Ground	The Shay
Biggest crowd	29,153 (v Wigan, in 1959)
Champions	Four times – 1903, 1907, 1965, 1986
Challenge Cup	Five times – 1903, 1904, 1931, 1939, 1987
Greatest moment	Beating St Helens in the 1987 Challenge Cup final by 19 points to 18, the year after they were champions.
Star man	Johnny Freeman, Welsh born winger who holds the club record for tries in a season (48) and career (290) between 1954 and 1967.
Amazing Fact	Before they joined the Northern Union in 1895, Halifax were one of the most successful rugby teams in the country. They won the Yorkshire Cup in 1878, in its first season and then won it a further four times before 1895. They also provided five England internationals during the same period.

HEMEL HEMSTEAD STAGS

Year Formed	1981
Old nickname	None
Ground	Pennine Way Sports Ground
Biggest crowd	679 (v Oldham in 2013)
Champions	Never
Challenge Cup	Never
Greatest moment	Winning the National Conference League Three championship in 2012 as a community club, the year before they became a professional club.
Star man	The Stags have seen several of their former players go on to join professional clubs, probably the most famous is Kieran Dixon, who is one of the top try scorers at London Broncos in the Super League.
Amazing Fact	The Stags really have built themselves up from nothing. When they first started in 1981 they had to borrow their kit but over the years the club has developed, and now has its own small stadium and several teams competing in different leagues in the south of England.

HUDDERSFIELD GIANTS

Year Formed	1863
Old nickname	Fartowners
Ground	John Smith's Stadium
Biggest crowd	32,912 (v Wigan in 1950)
Champions	Seven times – 1912, 1913, 1915, 1929, 1930, 1949, 1962
Challenge Cup	Six times – 1913, 1915, 1920, 1933, 1945, 1953
Greatest moment	Winning all four cups in 1915, the Huddersfield team were known as 'the team of all the talents'.
Star man	Harold Wagstaff, nick-named the prince of centres, was only 15 when he made his debut for Huddersfield in 1906. He captained Great Britain on two tours of Australia in 1914 and 1920.
Amazing Fact	When Harold Wagstaff signed on for Huddersfield in 1906, his signing on fee was £5! This was about three times the average weekly wage of a labourer at that time.

HULL FC

Year Formed	1865
Old nickname	Known as the Sharks for a short period, before reverting back to the 'Airlie Birds'
Ground	KC Stadium
Biggest crowd	28,798 (v Leeds in 1936)
Champions	Six times – 1920, 1921, 1936, 1956, 1958, 1983
Challenge Cup	Three times – 1914, 1982, 2005
Greatest moment	Winning the Challenge Cup in 1982 after beating Widnes in a replay at Elland Road, Leeds. The final had ended in a 14 all draw at Wembley.
Star man	Clive Sullivan, winger born in Wales, captained Great Britain to their world cup win in 1972. He was the first black captain of any British international team and scored over 200 tries for Hull, before transferring to Hull KR where he scored over 100 tries. He died aged just 42. The main road in to the city of Hull is the Clive Sullivan Way.
Amazing Fact	Hull FC were the last team to win the BBC Floodlit Trophy in 1979. This was a competition played on evenings with one match a week screened live on BBC TV. Hull beat Hull KR in the final.

HULL KINGSTON ROVERS

Year Formed	1883
Old nickname	Red Breasts
Ground	Craven Park
Biggest crowd	22,282 (v Hull in 1922)
Champions	Five times – 1923, 1925, 1979, 1984, 1985
Challenge Cup	Once - 1980
Greatest moment	Winning the Challenge Cup Final in 1980 beating arch rivals Hull FC, by 10 points to 5.
Star man	Roger Millward, a half back who joined Rovers from Castleford in 1966, making his last appearance in 1980. He then went on to coach the club for several seasons. He played more than 400 times for Rovers and scored more than 200 tries.
Amazing Fact	Hull Kingston Rovers played at the Boulevard Athletic grounds in the west of the city until 1895 when they moved to a new ground on the east side of the city. Hull FC moved into the Boulevard to replace them and this remained their stadium until 2002.

HUNSLET HAWKS

Year Formed	1883
Old nickname	Parksiders
Ground	South Leeds Stadium
Biggest crowd	24,700 (v Wigan in 1924)
Champions	Twice – 1908, 1938
Challenge Cup	Twice – 1908, 1934
Greatest moment	The first team to win all four trophies available to them in 1907/08. Their forward pack was known as the 'terrible six'.
Star man	Albert Goldthorpe, who made his debut at the age of 16 in 1888 playing full back. When he retired in 1910 he was the all-time leading scorer at the time, having kicked over 200 drop goals in his career.
Amazing Fact	Hunslet won the Championship in 1938, beating Leeds 8-2 in the final, the only time the final has been played between two clubs from Leeds. It was played at Elland Road, home of Leeds United and watched by over 54,000 people.

KEIGHLEY COUGARS

Year Formed	1901
Old nickname	None
Ground	Cougar Park (Lawkholme Lane)
Biggest crowd	14,500 (v Halifax in 1951)
Champions	Never
Challenge Cup	Never, finalists in 1937
Greatest moment	Reaching the Challenge Cup final in 1937, where they lost to Widnes.
Star man	Derek Hallas, a centre who signed for Keighley from a local rugby union side. He played for Leeds later in his career and also played for Great Britain twice in the early 1960s. He also had a short period at Parramatta in Australia.
Amazing Fact	Keighley were champions of the old division two in 1995, which would normally have guaranteed them promotion to the top division for the first time. However this coincided with the decision to move to summer rugby and Super League, reducing the number of clubs in the top division and Keighley were not promoted.

LEEDS RHINOS

Year Formed	1870
Old nickname	Loiners
Ground	Headingley Carnegie
Biggest crowd	40,175 (v Bradford in 1947)
Champions	Nine times – 1961, 1969, 1972, 2004, 2007, 2008, 2009, 2011, 2012
Challenge Cup	Ten times - 1910, 1923, 1932, 1936, 1941, 1942, 1957, 1968, 1977, 1978, 1999
Greatest moment	Winning the Super League title for the third consecutive season by beating St Helens in the final in 2009.
Star man	Eric Harris, an Australian who scored 391 tries in 383 games for Leeds, including 63 in season 1935/36.
Amazing Fact	Leeds' stadium, Headingley Carnegie is next door to the test cricket ground of the same name. Occasionally cricket and rugby have been played at the same time, but when a cricket test match is held there, the rugby pitch has been used for temporary bars and restaurants.

LEIGH CENTURIONS

Year Formed	1878
Old nickname	None
Ground	Leigh Sports Village
Biggest crowd	31,326 (v St Helens in 1953)
Champions	Twice – 1906, 1982
Challenge Cup	Twice – 1921, 1971
Greatest moment	Winning the championship in 1982 for only the second time in their history, led by their coach Alex Murphy.
Star man	John Woods, played over 300 games and scored over 2,000 points whilst at Leigh. He could play every position in the backs and gained international caps for both England and Great Britain.
Amazing Fact	Leigh moved into their new ground, Leigh Sporting Village, in late 2008 and share it with the Leigh Genesis Football club.

LONDON BRONCOS

Year Formed	1980
Old nickname	Crusaders
Ground	The Twickenham Stoop
Biggest crowd	15,013 (v Wakefield Trinity in 1981)
Champions	Never
Challenge Cup	Never – Finalists in 1999
Greatest moment	Beaten finalists against Leeds in the last Challenge Cup final to be played at the old Wembley in 1999.
Star man	Hussein M'Barki, former Moroccan rugby union player, signed for Fulham (as the Broncos were known as then) in 1982. A winger or centre he has been involved in the development of the game in his home country.
Amazing Fact	Broncos were originally formed as Fulham and have played at many stadiums across London including Craven Cottage, The Valley, Crystal Palace athletics stadium, Griffin Park and the Stoop.

LONDON SKOLARS

Year Formed	1995
Old nickname	The club was originally known as the Student Rugby League Old Boys
Ground	White Hart Lane Community Sports Centre
Biggest crowd	1,375 (v Oldham, 2010)
Champions	Never
Challenge Cup	Never
Greatest moment	In 2002, the Skolars were the first amateur club to successfully apply for a place in the professional rugby league for 80 years.
Star man	Joe Mbu, born in Zaire but brought up in London, a second row forward for a period with the Skolars before spending most of his professional career with the London Broncos. He then went on to be the head coach at the Skolars.
Amazing Fact	When the Skolars became professional in 2002 it was the first time since the 1930s that there has been two professional rugby league clubs in London.

NORTH WALES CRUSADERS

Year Formed	2005
Old nickname	Formerly known as 'Celtic' Crusaders
Ground	Racecourse Ground, Wrexham
Biggest crowd	10,334 (v Leeds in 2010)
Champions	Never, but did win the National League One title in 2007 and 2013.
Challenge Cup	Never
Greatest moment	Winning promotion to the Super League in 2008.
Star man	Gareth Thomas, made 100 appearances for Wales in rugby union before deciding to switch codes and play rugby league for the Crusaders. He played several times for the Welsh rugby league team in either the centre or on the wing.
Amazing Fact	The Crusaders were the result of years of hard work building up rugby league in south Wales, starting with amateur club Cardiff Demons in 1997 and resulting in enough players of a good standard to form a professional club in 2005.

OLDHAM

Year Formed	1876
Old nickname	Roughyeds
Ground	Whitebank Stadium
Biggest crowd	28,000 (v Huddersfield in 1912)
Champions	Four times – 1905, 1910, 1911, 1957,
Challenge Cup	Three times – 1899, 1925, 1927
Greatest moment	Beating Hull, the holders, in the 1957 Championship final.
Star man	Andy Goodway, a second rower, who played 11 times for Great Britain, including captaining them on tour whilst at Oldham before transferring to Wigan in 1985.
Amazing Fact	Oldham have never reached the Challenge Cup final at Wembley. During the 1980s and 1990s they lost four Challenge Cup semi-finals.

OXFORD RL

Year Formed	2012
Old nickname	None
Ground	Iffley Road Stadium
Biggest crowd	374 (v North Wales Crusaders in 2013)
Champions	Never
Challenge Cup	Never
Greatest moment	Acceptance as a professional club by the Rugby Football League, which means from 2013 they played in the Championship One.
Star man	2013 was Oxford RL's first professional season so picking a star man is difficult, however Darrell Griffin, the Salford City Reds prop forward did begin his career at his local rugby league club, Oxford Cavaliers.
Amazing Fact	Rugby has been played at Oxford RL's Iffley Road stadium since the 1890s when the Oxford Union Rugby Football Club bought the ground from Christ College for £1,000. Oxford University have played rugby league since 1976 but the Oxford RL club is a new club separate from the university and local community club Oxford Cavaliers.

ROCHDALE HORNETS

Year Formed	1871
Old nickname	Always the Hornets
Ground	Spotland
Biggest crowd	26,664 (v Oldham in 1922)
Champions	Never
Challenge Cup	Once - 1922
Greatest moment	The Hornets have only ever reached the Challenge Cup final once in 1922 when they won against Hull. They have therefore a 100% record in the Challenge Cup final, never beaten, not many clubs can claim that!
Star man	Bobbie Goulding, a scrum half who played at ten clubs during his career as well as for Great Britain ended his playing career at Rochdale as player coach. This was the start of his coaching career which included a period as the coach of the French national team.
Amazing Fact	Hornets' original ground, was the Athletics Ground and in the early 1900s it was compared with Headingley as one of the best grounds in the country. Therefore cup finals and semi-finals were held there with 41,000 packing in to it in 1924 for a Challenge Cup final. It gradually became dilapidated and Hornets had lots of debts, meaning it was sold and a supermarket was built on the site in 1989.

SALFORD RED DEVILS

Year Formed	1896
Old nickname	Red Devils – they return to this nickname in 2014
Ground	Salford City Stadium
Biggest crowd	26,470 (v Warrington in 1937)
Champions	Six – 1913, 1933, 1937, 1939, 1974, 1976
Challenge Cup	Once - 1938
Greatest moment	Salford were champions in seasons 1973/4 and 1975/6 and in the season in-between they won the Floodlit Trophy, the most successful period in the club's history.
Star man	David Watkins, a Welsh half-back, he scored over 3,000 points for Salford after signing from rugby union. He also captained the British and Irish Lions at rugby union and Great Britain in rugby league.
Amazing Fact	Salford take their nick-name from when they toured France in 1934. The French called them 'Les Diables Rouges de Salford' or the Red Devils of Salford. Sometime later near neighbours, Manchester United decided to take the same nick-name.

ST HELENS

Year Formed	1873
Old nickname	Rangers, now known as 'The Saints'
Ground	Langtree Park
Biggest crowd	35,695 (v Wigan in 1949)
Champions	Twelve – 1932, 1953, 1959, 1966, 1970, 1971, 1975, 1996, 1999, 2000, 2002, 2006
Challenge Cup	Twelve – 1956, 1961, 1966, 1972, 1976, 1996, 1997, 2001, 2004, 2006, 2007, 2008
Greatest moment	St Helens have been the most successful team of the Super League era and, in 2006, they did the 'double' of winning the Challenge Cup and the Super League in the same season. This helped them to become the 'team of the year' in the BBC TV sports awards for that year.
Star man	Tom Van Vollenhoven, a South African winger who holds the club record for tries in a career at 392. 62 of these came in the 1958/9 season.
Amazing Fact	St Helens moved in to their Knowsley Road ground in 1890. They played their last game there in 2010 moving in to their new stadium in 2012 after a temporary stay at Widnes during 2011.

SHEFFIELD EAGLES

Year Formed	1984
Old nickname	None
Ground	Don Valley Stadium (this stadium closed in September 2013 with a new stadium to be built on the site, in the meantime it is likely the Eagles will play at their original home at Owlerton Stadium).
Biggest crowd	10,603 (v Bradford in 1997)
Champions	Never
Challenge Cup	Once - 1998
Greatest moment	Without doubt winning the Challenge Cup final in 1998. The Eagles were given no chance against the mighty Wigan but ran out victors by 17-8.
Star man	Mark Aston, scrum half who was the man of the match in the cup final in 1998. He holds the club record for most goals and points in a career at the Eagles; he has coached the team and is now the Chief Executive (the boss) of the club. And in between all that he also played for Great Britain.
Amazing Fact	Sheffield Eagles were the last side to be beaten in a Yorkshire Cup final in 1992. After this season it was decided there was not enough time in the fixture list to play county cup competitions.

SOUTH WALES SCORPIONS

Year Formed	2009
Old nickname	None
Ground	The Gnoll, Neath
Biggest crowd	890 (v Swinton in 2009)
Champions	Never
Challenge Cup	Never
Greatest moment	Gaining entry to the professional rugby league as the second professional club in Wales and reaching the Championship One play-offs in their first season.
Star man	Gil Dudson, the Wigan and Wales prop forward spent a season playing for the Scorpions in 2010.
Amazing Fact	Former coach Anthony Seibold is probably one of the most travelled rugby league players, he played professional rugby league in four different countries before becoming a coach. As well as playing for Canberra Raiders and Brisbane Broncos in his native Australia, he played for St Esteve (France), London Broncos and Hull KR (England) before ending his playing career with the Crusaders (Wales).

SWINTON LIONS

Year Formed	1866
Old nickname	Always 'The Lions'
Ground	Leigh Sports Village
Biggest crowd	26,891 (v Wigan in 1964)
Champions	Six times – 1927, 1928, 1931, 1935, 1963, 1964
Challenge Cup	Three times – 1900, 1926, 1928
Greatest moment	The last club to perform the feat of winning all four cups in one season in 1927/8 season.
Star man	Martin Hodgson, a goal kicking second row forward he toured with Great Britain to Australasia in 1932 and 1936. He also represented the county of his birth, Cumberland.
Amazing Fact	Danny Wilson was a Welsh international stand-off who played for Swinton in the 1980s. His son is also a Welsh international and perhaps a little more famous - Ryan Giggs, the Manchester United player.

WAKEFIELD TRINITY WILDCATS

Year Formed	1873
Old nickname	Dreadnoughts
Ground	Rapid Solicitors Stadium (Belle Vue)
Biggest crowd	28,254 (v Wigan in 1962)
Champions	Twice – 1967, 1968
Challenge Cup	Five times – 1909, 1946, 1960, 1962, 1963
Greatest moment	Winning the Challenge Cup against Wigan in 1963 which meant they won the trophy three times in four years. Over the same period they were runners up in two Championship finals, a win in either would have secured the 'double'.
Star man	Neil Fox, a centre who was also a goal kicker, he scored a rugby league record of over 6,000 points in his career, over 4,000 of them whilst at Wakefield. He also played 29 times for Great Britain.
Amazing Fact	In 1963 'This Sporting Life' was an Oscar nominated movie based on the book of the same name by David Storey. It starred famous actors Richard Harris and Rachel Roberts and was about the life of a rugby league player. Many of the scenes in the film were filmed at Belle Vue, Wakefield's ground.

WARRINGTON WOLVES

Year Formed	1879
Old nickname	Wire
Ground	Halliwell Jones Stadium
Biggest crowd	34,304 (v Wigan in 1949)
Champions	Three times – 1948, 1954, 1955
Challenge Cup	Eight times - 1905, 1907, 1950, 1954, 1974, 2009, 2010, 2012
Greatest moment	Retaining the Challenge Cup in 2010, with a victory over Leeds Rhinos in the final at Wembley.
Star man	Brian Bevan, an Australian born winger who played for Warrington from 1945 to 1962. During his career he scored an amazing 796 tries, the vast majority for Warrington.
Amazing Fact	When Warrington met Halifax in the Challenge Cup final replay at Odsal in 1954, it was in front of a then world record crowd of 102,569. The two teams met again only three days later in the Championship final (the Grand Final as we would know it) at Maine Road in Manchester where the crowd was just 36,519. Warrington won that game as well to complete the 'double'.

WHITEHAVEN

Year Formed	1948
Old nickname	Haven
Ground	The Recreation Ground
Biggest crowd	18,500 (v Wakefield in 1960)
Champions	Never
Challenge Cup	Never
Greatest moment	In 1956 Whitehaven not only beat the touring Australian side but also got as far as the Challenge Cup semi-final, only to lose to Leeds by one point. In 2005 Whitehaven finished top of the Championship and won the league leaders shield, however they were beaten by Castleford in the grand final, the second year in succession they had lost out on promotion in this way.
Star man	John McKeown, a full back, holds the record for most points, most goals and most appearances in a career for Whitehaven. He played between 1948 and 1961 and also represented Great Britain and Cumberland.
Amazing Fact	Although Whitehaven were not formed until 1948 the Recreation Ground existed for many years before this and rugby matches had been staged on it during this time. The most notable being Whitehaven Recreation (what we would now describe as an amateur or community club) who beat St Helens there in a Challenge Cup match in 1908.

WIDNES VIKINGS

Year Formed	1873
Old nickname	The Chemics
Ground	Select Security Stadium (Naughton Park)
Biggest crowd	24,205 (v St Helens in 1961)
Champions	Three times – 1978, 1988, 1989
Challenge Cup	Seven times – 1930, 1937, 1964, 1975, 1979, 1981, 1984
Greatest moment	During the 1970s Widnes became known as the cup kings as they seemed to be in every cup final during that decade. In 1978/9 Widnes won three of the smaller trophies, (Lancashire cup, Floodlit Trophy and Premiership) and also the Challenge Cup at Wembley against Wakefield Trinity.
Star man	Martin Offiah. A London born winger, Offiah was one of many rugby union players coach Doug Laughton brought to Widnes in the late 1980s. He scored over 180 tries for Widnes before moving to Wigan.
Amazing Fact	In 1986, Widnes looked at the idea of having artificial turf (grass made out of a type of plastic) at their ground; however, at the time it was not suitable to play rugby on. Widnes do now play on artificial grass as it has now been developed to play rugby on.

WIGAN WARRIORS

Year Formed	1879
Old nickname	Wasps
Ground	DW Stadium
Biggest crowd	47,747 (v St Helens in 1959)
Champions	Twenty times - 1909, 1922, 1926, 1934, 1946, 1947, 1950, 1952, 1960, 1987, 1990, 1991, 1992, 1993, 1994, 1995, 1996, 1998, 2010, 2013.
Challenge Cup	Nineteen times – 1924, 1929, 1948, 1951, 1958, 1959, 1965, 1985, 1988, 1989, 1990, 1991, 1992, 1993, 1994, 1995, 2002, 2011, 2013
Greatest moment	The most successful rugby league club of all time, Wigan dominated the game during the late 1980s and the early 1990s, winning the Championship six consecutive years from 1990 to 1995.
Star man	There are many contenders but Jim Sullivan, a Welsh goal kicking full back, still holds the club's points scoring record over a career despite all the successes of the late twentieth century. He scored almost 5,000 points whilst at Wigan between 1921 and 1940.
Amazing Fact	The 1948 Challenge Cup final between Wigan and Bradford was the first to be televised, although few in Wigan would have watched it as it was only broadcast live to the midlands of England by the BBC.

WORKINGTON TOWN

Year Formed	1945
Old nickname	None
Ground	Derwent Park
Biggest crowd	17,741 (v Wigan in 1965)
Champions	Once - 1951
Challenge Cup	Once - 1952
Greatest moment	During the 1950s Town were one of the top sides, winning the Championship in 1951 and the Challenge Cup in 1952, as well as being beaten finalists at Wembley in 1955 and 1958.
Star man	Gus Risman, a Welsh full-back or centre. He joined Workington as player coach late in his career and was aged 41 when he led Town to win the Challenge Cup in 1952. The Great Britain international scored more than 1,500 points whilst playing with Workington.
Amazing Fact	Workington played in the first season of Super League. Unfortunately they only won two games and were relegated.

YORK CITY KNIGHTS

Year Formed	1901
Old nickname	Wasps
Ground	Huntington Stadium
Biggest crowd	14,689 (v Swinton in 1934)
Champions	Never
Challenge Cup	Never
Greatest moment	York were champions of the old division two in 1980/1, gaining promotion to the top division. They finished above Wigan and Fulham (now London Broncos) two current Super League clubs, who were also promoted, in that season
Star man	Many players have begun their career at York before going on to play at a higher level. Stand-off Graham Steadman started his career at York before making his name at Castleford, where he was also a Great Britain international and eventually a coach.
Amazing Fact	Former player coach Chris Thorman was born in Newcastle and has two brothers who are also professional rugby league players. Paul and Neil have played for London Skolars and Gateshead Thunder. Chris holds the world record for the fastest ever hat-trick of tries in either code of rugby when he played at Huddersfield – taking just under seven minutes against Doncaster in 2002.

Were you paying attention?

Let's test your rugby league knowledge and your ability to find information with the following twenty questions. All the answers are in this section on clubs and the number of points for answering the question is in brackets.

1   How many times have Featherstone Rovers won the Challenge Cup? *(1 point)*

2   What is the last name of the three brothers born in Newcastle who played rugby league for three different clubs? *(1 point)*

3   What is the name of Whitehaven's stadium? *(1 point)*

4   Add the number of times Batley Bulldogs have won the Challenge Cup with the number of times Leigh Centurions have been champions. Multiply the answer by the number of times Oldham have won the Challenge Cup. *(2 points)*

5   Which club were originally known as the 'Student Rugby League Old Boys'? *(1 point)*

6   How many times have Wigan won the Challenge Cup? *(1 point)*

7   Which club were formed in 2009 and play home games in Neath? *(1 point)*

8   Which club were originally known as Fulham when they were first formed? *(1 point)*

9   Which club's stadium is next door to a cricket ground that has the same name? *(1 point)*

10 Gus Risman was 41 years old when he captained which club in the Challenge Cup final? *(2 points)*

11 Who play at the Halliwell Jones Stadium? *(1 point)*

12 Which club did Martin Offiah score over 180 tries for before moving to Wigan? *(1 point)*

13 Ryan Giggs' dad played for which team in the 1980s? *(1 point)*

14 Which team were formed after a merger between St Esteve and XIII Catalan? *(1 point)*

15 How many times have these teams won the
Challenge Cup? *(1 point for each)*
a) Castleford
b) Hull Kingston Rovers
c) Widnes Vikings

16 Which club pulled off the biggest shock in Challenge
Cup history by beating Wigan in the final in 1998? *(1 point)*

17 Who beat Wests Tigers in 2006 to win the World Club
Challenge for the third time? *(1 point)*

18 Michael 'Stevo' Stephenson (the Sky TV commentator)
played for which team that won the championship in
1973? *(1 point)*

19 Welsh rugby union legend Gareth Thomas played
rugby league for which team? *(1 point)*

20 Two teams have a home stadium called Craven Park.
who are they? *(1 point for each)*

Turn over for the Answers

1 Three times - 1967, 1973, 1983
2 Thorman
3 The Recreation Ground
4 Batley have won the Challenge Cup
three times, Leigh have been Champions
twice and Oldham have won the Challenge
Cup three times. So 3+2=5 x3= 15
5 London Skolars
6 19 times
7 South Wales Scorpions
8 London Broncos
9 Leeds Rhinos - Headingley

10 Workington Town
11 Warrington Wolves
12 Widnes
13 Swinton Lions
14 Catalan Dragons
15 Castleford - 4, Hull KR - 1, Widnes - 7
16 Sheffield Eagles
17 Bradford Bulls
18 Dewsbury
19 North Wales Crusaders
20 Hull KR and Barrow Raiders

How did you do?

20 to 25 points – wow, did you write this book?

15 to 20 points – Your rugby league knowledge is very good.

10 to 15 points – Not bad, perhaps take some time to re-read some of
the facts and have another go!

5 to 10 points – Oh dear, it's the sixth tackle and you are still only
twenty metres from your own line, you need something special to
improve on that score.

Less than 5 points – Did you read this chapter or just come straight to
the quiz? Go back and read the whole book again!

Bibliography
(or the books I looked in to get some of the information for this book)

'Rugby League, an Illustrated History' Robert Gate

'1895 and All That...Inside Rugby League's Hidden History' Tony Collins

'The Grounds of Rugby League' Trevor Delaney

'The Forbidden Game' Mike Rylance

'Champagne Rugby' Henri Garcia

'The Rugby League Miscellany' David Lawrenson

'The Glory of Their Times' Phil Melling and Tony Collins

'At the George' Geoffrey Moorhouse

'Harold Bowman on Tour Down Under' Micheal Ulyatt and David Bowman

'Longy' Sean Long with Nick Appleyard

'Daydream believer' Stanley Gene with Stuart Wilkin

Gillette Rugby League Yearbook 2010

The clubs' official websites